Princess and Frog

Fairytale Writing Adventure

For every girl who wants to be a princess

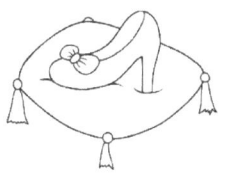

Jan May

New Millennium Girl Books &

New Millennium School Books – Language Arts

Princess and Frog Fairytale Writing Adventure

by Jan May

Copyright 2022, Jan May

Education and Language Arts

All rights reserved. No part of this book may be shared, given away, or reproduced for sale in any manner whatsoever.

Printed in the United States of America

ISBN 978-1-7321119-3-6

Published by New Millennium Girl Books

690 Laurel Drive

Aurora, IL 60506

Clipart by

Kate Hadfield Designs https://katehadfielddesigns.com/
Artifex https://www.teacherspayteachers.com/Store/Artifex

Welcome to Princess and Frog Fairytale Writing Adventure

This is a fun creative writing curriculum designed to eliminate work for the teacher. It is user-friendly for grades 3-6 with simple, self-guided step-by-step instructions. There are twelve easy lessons with several worksheets and activities for each lesson. This curriculum can be used in your individual homeschool or with a group. It's also a great summer project.

Each lesson is designed to last 45-60 minutes and has four sections:
- Lesson Time
- Writing Time
- Activity Time
- Princess School Time - *Focus on Inner Beauty*

Whether your student is a skilled writer or just starting out, this curriculum will inspire a love for writing. The fun activities and optional crafts in each lesson will keep your students happily busy for hours. The course will culminate at the end of twelve weeks with a story and Fairytale Flashlight Theater. This book teaches:

- How to develop a character, setting, and plot
- How to write a story with a moral
- Choosing a theme that encourages character growth
- How to spice up your dialogue with adjectives
- How to incorporate literary tools like personification and *Show, Don't Tell*, the golden rule of writing

Introduction - Teacher's Notes

I have taught creative writing for over fifteen years and have found that given the right tools, any child can learn to write and love it. I always stress creativity over grammar, and I praise every small effort made. I encourage parents to use the five writing superpowers for success as described on the next page. The brainstorming and fun activities for each lesson create a "writing adventure" instead of a dull writing lesson. I have discovered that keeping these things in mind, even the most reluctant writer will dive into the writing pool!

Fairytales and fables are fun to read and can teach us good life lessons. Some examples of good lessons are:

> "The Grasshopper and the Ant" – Hard work and preparation pay off.

- The three little pigs learn that the easiest way isn't always the best way. Laziness will leave you poor.

- Mulan learns that heroes come in all shapes and sizes.

- Beauty learns that kindness can kill a beast and appearances can be deceiving.

- Pinocchio learns to obey his parents, be honest, and be brave.

Check out my Pinterest page for more fun princess crafts: https://www.pinterest.com/janmay2012/princess-fun/

Get the Most out of These Lessons by Using The Five Writing Superpowers

Brainstorming - Never underestimate the creative power of brainstorming! Talking things out with your students helps to form ideas and primes the pump of creativity. Continue asking them about their characters and brainstorming ideas throughout the lessons. This also creates excitement when they can share their ideas with you. This begins the writing adventure!

Prewriting – This can be anything from writing down simple ideas to organizing thoughts on a list. Each prewriting activity helps the student formulate the story and organize their thoughts. It's like constructing a building in the students' minds so when it's time to put pencil on paper they have tons of ideas to draw from.

Freewriting- Write down whatever comes into a person's mind. Let your students write about what they love - zany plots, quirky characters, made-up fantasy worlds, and all. This will unleash the storyteller in your child, and if they have been "stuck" it will open the floodgates for writing.

Gentle Grading - Don't make creative writing a lesson in grammar or spelling. Children will feel stifled if they have to stop and sound out every word and fear that you will mark it wrong. Let them have a good start first and feel confident, then begin correcting after a time, *gently*. This could easily be after a month or two. Introduce grammar and writing rules one at a time so they can build mastery before going on to a new rule.

Theme Immersion – Give your students fun activities that immerse them in the theme they are writing about. This creates a rich atmosphere that nourishes the imagination and creates a fun writing adventure that will springboard them into writing.

Contents

Introduction - Teacher's Notes . . . 4

Five Writing Superpowers of Success . . . 5

Lesson One - Create a Fairytale Character . . . 9

    Create a Character Handout . . . 10

    Princess School – *Be a Follower of God's Word* . . . 13

    Activity – Make a Princess School Diary . . . 14

Lesson Two - Develop Story Ideas . . . 17

    Plot your Story . . . 21

    Princess School – *Thankfulness is Beautiful* . . . 23

    Activity – Make a Princess Paper Doll . . . 24

Lesson Three - Create a Sensory Setting . . . 31

    Princess School – *Kindness is Beautiful* . . . 33

    Activity – Make a Fairytale Backdrop Poster . . . 37

Lesson Four - Write the Beginning . . . 43

    Begin your Story with Four Important Elements . . . 43

    Princess School – *Courage is Beautiful* . . . 46

    Activity – Draw a Scene . . . 47

Lesson Five - Create Dialogue . . . 48

    How to Write Interesting Dialogue . . . 49

    Comic Strip Handout . . . 50

    Princess School – *Forgiving is Beautiful* . . . 53

    Activity – Make Princess Hats . . . 54

Lesson Six - Show, Don't Tell . . . 55

    Handout Practice – Showing Emotions . . . 56

    Princess School – *Believe in Yourself* . . . 58

    Activity – Make a Special Name Banner . . . 59

Lesson Seven - Write the Middle . . . 63

    How to Create Tension . . . 65

    Activity – Make Friendship Bracelets . . . 69

    Princess School – *Honesty is Beautiful*. . . 70

Lesson Eight - Use Personification . . . 71

    Continue Writing . . . 73

    Princess School – *Generosity is Beautiful* . . . 72

    Activity – Share your Time, Talents, and Treasures . . . 75

Lesson Nine - Spice Up Your Story with Adjectives . . . 76

    Activity – Write for the *Fairytale Gazette* . . . 80

    Princess School – *Diligence is Beautiful* . . . 79

Lesson Ten - Write the Ending . . . 83

    Activity – Illustrate a Scene from Your Story . . . 83

    Princess School – *Thinking of Others is Beautiful* . . . 84

    Write and Finish Your Story . . . 85

Lesson Eleven - Edit Your Story . . . 87

    Princess School – *Hospitality is Beautiful* . . . 88

    Activity – Bake Princess Cupcakes . . . 89

Lesson Twelve - Put It All Together . . . 90

    Fairytale Flashlight Theater . . . 90

Title Page Cover Template . . . 91

Extra Fairytale Writing Paper . . . 95

About the Author . . . 107

Lesson One
Create a Fairytale Character

Lesson Time

Fairytales and fables are fun to read and can teach us good life lessons. The first thing to do when starting a fairytale is to create an interesting character that you will enjoy reading about. In this story, you will create a princess character.

A good story helps a character grow. She should have a few weaknesses to be realistic. If the character starts out selfish, give her opportunities to learn how to give. If she is fearful, give her a situation where she learns to face her fears and gain courage. If she struggles with shyness, give her a situation when she has to be outgoing or bold to save someone's life or keep someone safe.

Writing Time

You will begin with some pre-writing activities. That means you will first write down ideas and plan your story for the next several chapters. This is an important step! First, fill out the handout on the next several pages called "Create a Fairytale Character." This will help you create the character that you will be writing about. You can change the answers if you get better ideas in the future.

Create a Fairytale Character

Name your character_____

How old is she? _____

What are her favorite hobbies?
_____

Describe what she looks like.
_____
_____
_____
_____

What is her favorite princess snack?
_____

What is her favorite subject at princess school?
_____

What is her favorite thing to do?
_____

Write down ideas that might be fun to write about with your character:

_____
_____
_____
_____

What is the name of the kingdom she lives in?
_____

Does she have any dreams for her life other than being a princess? What are they?

_____
_____
_____
_____

What does your character fear the most?

_____

What are some of her weaknesses?

_____
_____
_____
_____

What motivates her and gets her excited?

_____
_____
_____
_____
_____

Describe her family – the king, queen, and siblings.

_____
_____
_____
_____

Describe her best friend.

_____
_____
_____
_____

Draw a picture of your princess in the box below.

Princess School ⭐ 1

Following God's Word is Beautiful!

It's far easier to look beautiful on the outside, with shiny hair, sparkly jewelry, and pretty dresses. It's a lot harder to be beautiful on the inside. We have to work at it. The best book that shows us how to be beautiful on the inside is the Bible. It's filled with truth and life. When we follow what it says, our faces will shine with beauty from the inside out!

Copy the Bible Verse:

Proverbs 31:30, "Charm is deceptive, and beauty is fleeting, but a woman who fears the LORD is to be praised." (NIV)

_____

_____

_____

_____

Princess Homework

Make an itty-bitty "Princess School Diary" on the next page.

Activity Time - Make an Itty-Bitty "Princess School Diary"

You will need:

- 4 white or brown paper bags *about* 4.25 x 8 inches
- 1 piece of colored construction paper
- 1 - 4.25 x 8-inch piece of felt in fun pink, purple, or other colors of your choice
- 1 - 20-inch piece of .5-inch ribbon - the color of your choice
- 1 to 4 Styrofoam flowers, jewel embellishments, or glitter letters

Directions:

- With the paper bags closed flat, fold the paper bags in half then lay them on top of each other.

- With liquid glue, glue one folded half of one bag to the other folder half of the other bag. Do this to all four bags so that they form one book. DO NOT GLUE THE POCKETS CLOSED.

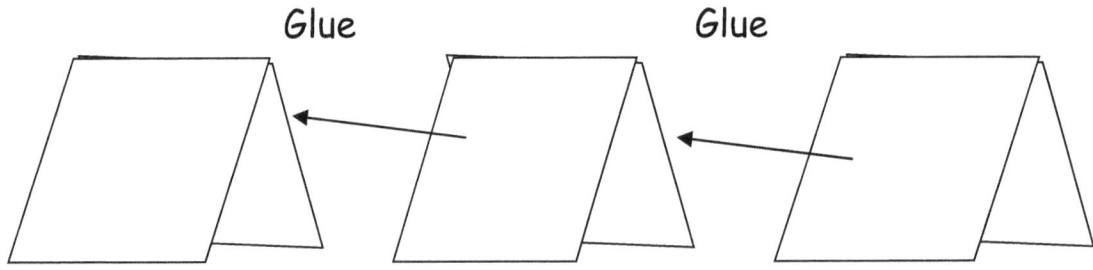

- With the bags open and laid flat, glue the ribbon around the center of the book, leaving 5-6 inches hanging off each side. Ribbon

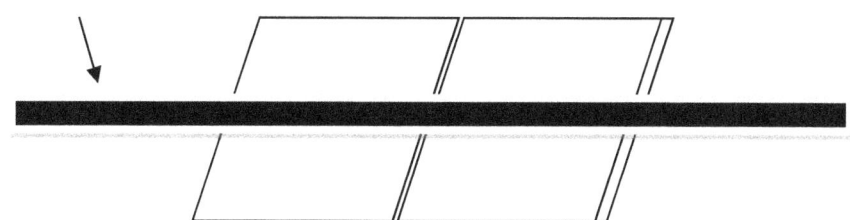

- Glue the felt-on top of the ribbon and bag, making a book cover. Match up the ends so all the paper bag is covered. Leave the 5-6 inches of ribbon hanging off. You can use this to tie both ends of the ribbon together to close the book.

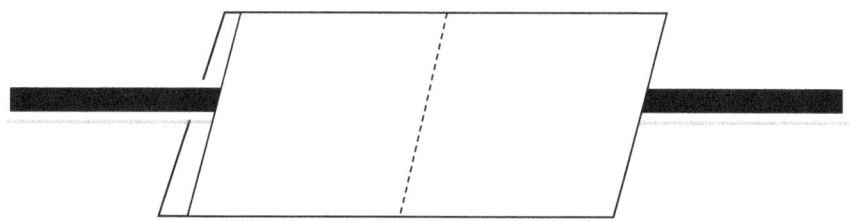

- Embellish the cover with flowers, jewels, or glitter. You could even make a glitter crown for the princess.

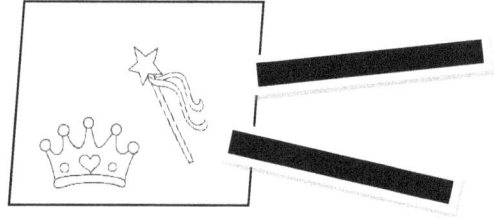

To make itty-bitty books to go inside each pocket:

- Cut four 4 x 8-inch pieces each of construction paper and white paper. Fold in half. Slip 4 pieces of white paper inside the construction paper cover.
- Label the 4 books: Princess Journal #1
  - Princess Journal #2
  - My Thankful Book
  - I am Special
- Slip one book inside each pocket of the bigger book.
- Tie closed.

You will write in the Princess School Diary throughout this curriculum.

Lesson Two
Developing Story Ideas

Lesson Time

A theme is the main idea that your story is about. Choose a theme that will help your characters grow and learn a good lesson. Here are some ideas for themes.

Patience - Learning to trust God's timing

When we pray for patience, God doesn't send us a basket full of patience, but He gives us opportunities to grow in patience. Usually, it comes with a difficult situation that forces us to use our faith muscles.

The Bible tells us in the book of James to consider it joyful when you must put up with hard situations, knowing that they create patience in us. (James 1:2-3)

Make a list of some things that a person might have to be patient about. Some examples are: A princess is impatient to live a dream she has, or a young girl is impatient to grow up. Maybe the princess wants to be a dancer or a baker instead of a princess.

Write your ideas on the lines below:

_____
_____
_____
_____

Courage - Learning to trust God's protection

Courage isn't the absence of fear, but the ability to do what's right even though we are afraid.

The Bible says, "God has not given us a spirit of fear, but of love, power and a sound mind."   (2 Timothy 1:7)

He also says that He will never leave us, so we know that we can rely on His strength to help us in our time of need. This is what David remembered when he faced Goliath. Some ideas for courage may be that a princess sees someone doing wrong and must stand up for what is right. Maybe a princess may not want to become queen and runs away. Maybe she is afraid of snakes.

Make a list of things a person in a fairytale might be afraid of on the lines below.

_____
_____
_____
_____
_____

After reading these character qualities, you should have some good ideas for writing a story. Use the diagram on the next page to develop your ideas.

Writing Time - A

Write on the line below the lesson you want your character to learn.
_____

Use the story web below to create a problem that will help your character learn that lesson. Start by writing the lesson you want her to learn in the box above the princess' head. Then write whatever ideas pop into your mind to help her learn the lesson in one of the clouds. Keep going until all the clouds are filled. You can also add more clouds if you want to. For example, on my sheet, I chose "bravery" and wrote that in the middle square. Then I added story ideas to help her overcome her fears in the clouds like she must swim across a river to save someone's life, even though she is afraid of water, thus helping her conquer her fear.

Writing Time - B

Writing a Plot

A fairytale plot is like writing your own recipe. Start with a character who needs to learn something, add a few obstacles to keep her from getting it too soon, mix in some fun antics along the way, and help her reach her goal at the end.

It's a lot like a roller coaster ride. First, you climb up the roller coaster, then you slide down, then you go upside down and twist around before you finally reach the bottom. It's thrilling!

The way to accomplish this is to increase the tension by *almost* letting the character solve her problem but letting her fail on the first attempt. The story gets even more exciting if she fails twice. Some writers use the 1, 2, 3, method: the first two times fail, and on the third try the character succeeds and learns her lesson.

Prewriting Activity

Fill out the handout called "Plot Out Your Fairytale" on the next few pages. Use a pencil so you can change the ideas when better ones come to you.

Plot Out Your Fairytale in the Boxes

It all begins here with your character. Describe her.

Next, tell about the story problem.

How does your princess character try to solve the problem?

Does your princess character succeed in solving the problem or does the problem get worse?

What happens next?

What happens next?

What happens next?

End the story and help your character solve the problem.

Princess School ⭐2

Thankfulness is Beautiful!

Being thankful is a powerful thing, especially when things are going wrong. It helps us to focus on what God is doing instead of focusing on what is going wrong in our lives. This gives us a BIGGER PICTURE to think about and gives us hope that things will not always be difficult.

Copy the verse below:

1 Thessalonians 5:18, "In everything give thanks; for this is the will of God for you in Christ Jesus." (NIV)

_____
_____
_____
_____

Princess Homework

In your Princess School Diary, inside the book "My Thankful Book," write down five things you are thankful for today. Maybe it's something like sunshine or when someone did something nice for you. Add more things you are thankful for during the semester whenever something nice happens. By the end of this book, you will have a whole book filled with good things.

Activity Time - Make Princess Paper Dolls for Role Playing Your Story

- On the following pages, color the characters of your choice.

- Cut them out.

- Using a glue stick, glue them onto a file folder or a piece of light cardstock to make them sturdy. Cut them out.

- Cut out the stands for each paper doll.

- Cut the dotted lines and fold the stands in half.

- Insert the doll to make them stand up.

- You can role-play your story with them!

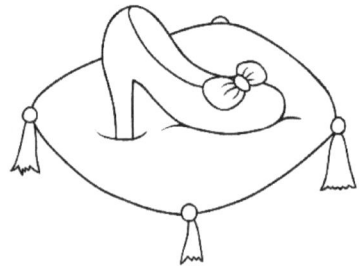

Horse Stand

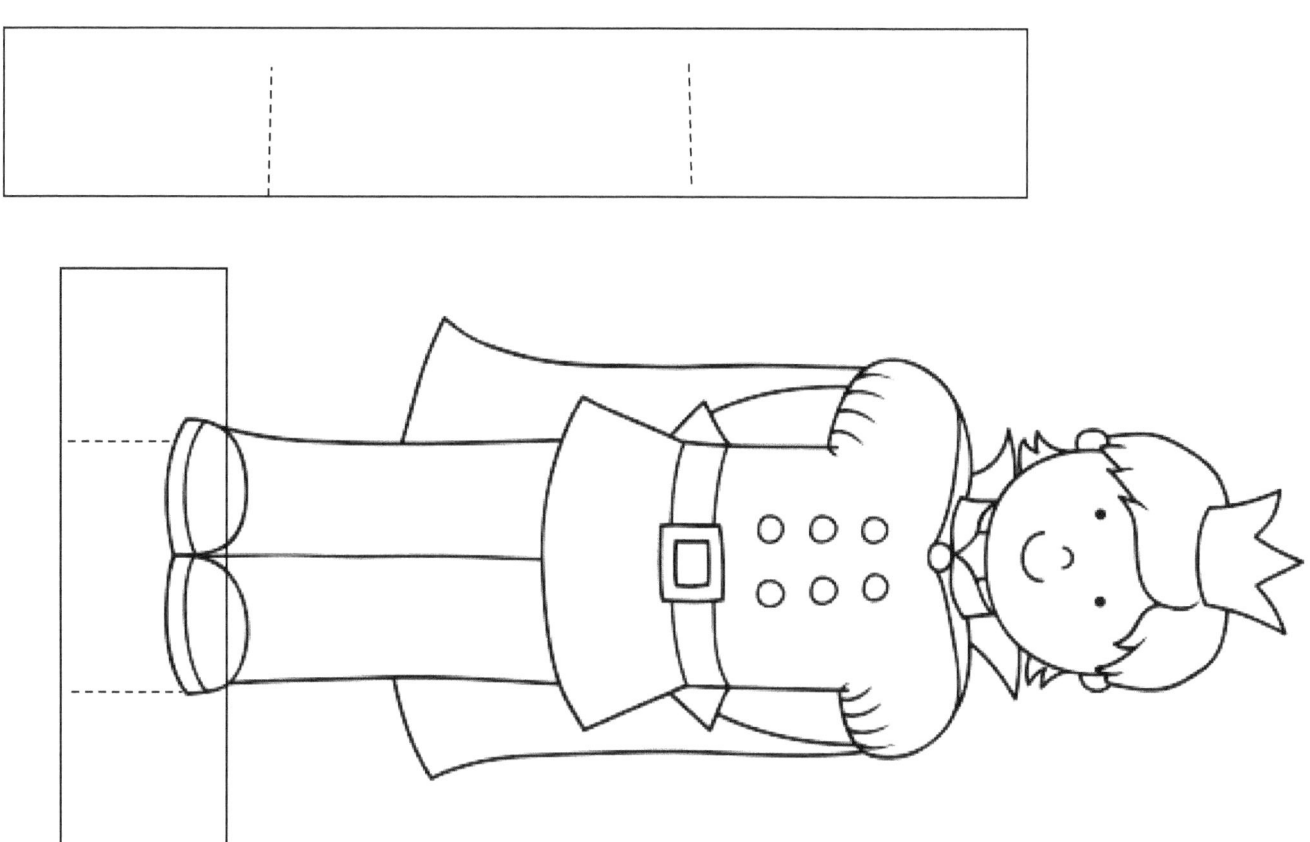
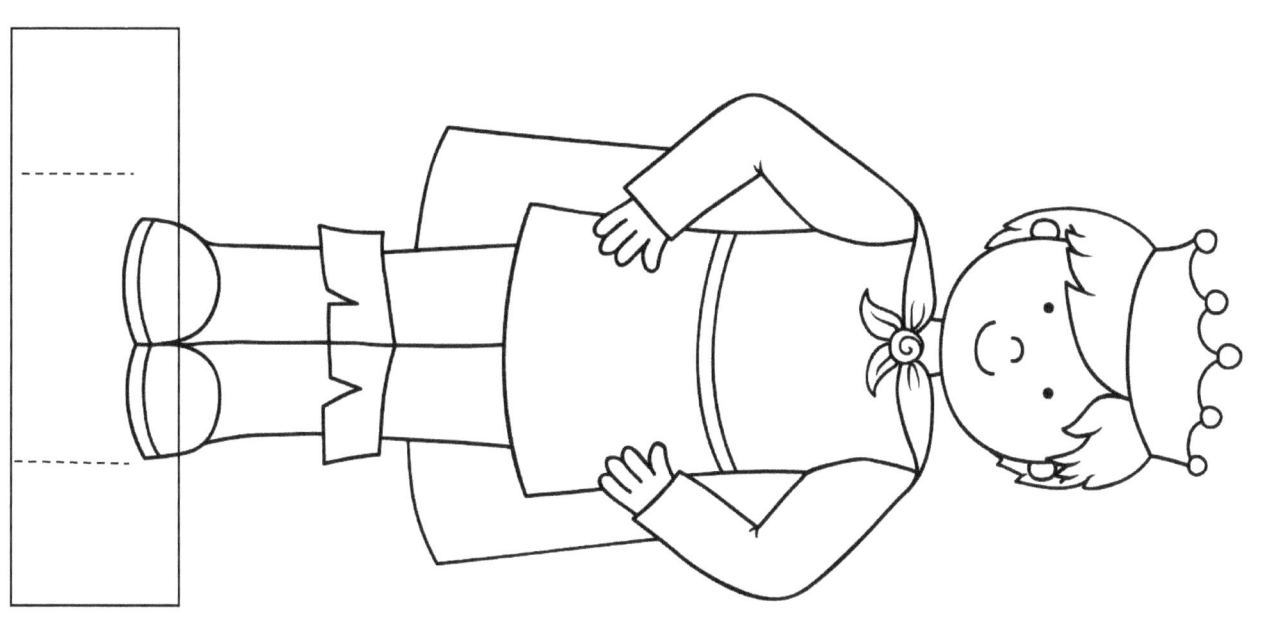

Lesson Three
Create a Sensory Setting

Lesson Time

A setting is the place and time in history where your story happens. Fairytale settings usually have castles, forests, villages, markets, and farms.

Describing the setting in your story helps paint a backdrop for your story, much like setting the stage for a play.

Using adjectives, words that describe, makes your writing come alive.

Which sentence is more interesting?

1. The forest was filled with animals. OR
2. The **magical** forest was filled with **talking** animals.

Sentence two gives a better picture in your imagination than sentence one because of the use of adjectives.

Writing Time

What setting are you going to use for your story? A magic forest? A village or castle? Something else? Write it here:

_____

Go to the next page and fill in the blanks about your setting.

Create a Setting Handout

It's important to describe the setting with colors, sights, and sounds. Use all your senses. Make a list below:

Sights include colors:

Example: yellow buttercups

_____

_____

_____

_____

Sounds include adjectives:

Example: bubbling brook

_____

_____

_____

_____

Smells include adjectives:

Example: sweet jasmine perfume

_____

_____

_____

_____

Things with texture:

Example: rough cobblestone road

_____

_____

_____

_____

Tastes include adjectives: *Example: warm cinnamon buns*

_____

_____

_____

_____

Princess School #3 – *Kindness is Beautiful!*

Our lips are the most beautiful when we speak with kind words. Being empathetic means we understand how the other person feels. Ask yourself, "What would I need if I felt the same way?" Then put on the lip gloss of kindness!

Copy the Bible verse:

Proverbs 16:24, "Kind words are like honey, sweet to the soul and healthy for the body." (NIV)

_____
_____
_____
_____
_____

Princess Homework

Use the notecards on page 35 and find two people to write a kind note for to cheer them up.

Draw the setting with a castle, trees, and horses.

Activity Time – Make a Fairytale Backdrop Poster

Make a fairytale poster as a background for your paper dolls. Color and cut out the pictures on pages 39 – 41. Using a glue stick, glue them onto a piece of white poster board. You can draw grass, sky, trees, birds, and flowers around your pictures.

Fill in the text boxes below to reflect the Bible verse. Then color the picture.

"Be kind and compassionate to one another, forgiving each other, just as in Christ God forgave you. Follow God's example, therefore, as dearly loved children and walk in the way of love, just as Christ loved us and gave himself up for us as a fragrant offering and sacrifice to God." Ephesians 4:32-33 NIV

Lesson Four
Begin Writing Your Story

Lesson Time - Every story has three major parts: a beginning, middle, and end. The beginning should have four important things, which are listed below. Answer these three questions to kickstart your beginning.

1. Introduce your main character.

_____
_____
_____

2. Describe the setting of your story. Where does it happen? Include what your setting looks like, sounds like, smells like, tastes like, and feels like.

_____
_____
_____

3. Tell about the story problem.

_____
_____
_____

4. Hook your readers by beginning your story in the middle of action. Write a hook below for your story. You can always change it later if you have a better idea.

_____
_____
_____

Help the princess by coloring her accessories.

Rewrite the sentences you wrote on page 43 to help you start your story. Then continue writing your story for 15-20 minutes. Skip a line. It makes it easier to edit later.

Princess School #4 – Courage is Beautiful!

Have you ever been with someone who is so timid that they couldn't do the right thing? Courage is taking a depth breath, asking God for help, then doing the right thing anyway. God promises to always be with you! You still might feel afraid but do the right thing anyway.

Copy the verse below.

2 Timothy 1:7 "For God has not given us a spirit of fear, but of power, and of love, and of a sound mind." (NKJV)

_____
_____
_____
_____

Princess Homework

Ask two people about a time they had to be brave and write about it in your journal.

Lesson Five
Dialogue

Lesson Time

Dialogue makes a story come alive because someone in your story is talking. Always include dialogue in your story by using quotation marks at the beginning, when your characters first start talking, and again at the end, when they are finished. Put all ending punctuation marks (like periods, question marks, or exclamation marks) *inside* the quotation marks.

Example:

"Race you to the castle!" said Princess Patty.

There are two parts to a sentence of dialogue. The first part is the quote (what the character actually said). The second part is the dialogue tag, telling who said it. You separate them with a comma unless you use an exclamation or question mark.

Example:

"Race you to the castle!" is the quotation.

Said Princess Patty is the dialogue tag.

What other dialogue tag could you use in that same sentence above?

Example: Instead of using "said" in the above example, you can write "Race you to the castle!" **shouted** Princess Patty.

Go on and read the next page.

Other Ways to Say "Said"

There are better ways to said. Circle 10 interesting dialogue tags below to use in your writing this week. Then go on to the next page and fill in the Comic Strip. Then write 15-20 minutes of your story.

admitted
agreed
answered
argued
asked
barked
begged
boasted
boomed
bragged
bellowed
blurted
complained
confessed
cried
defended
declared
demanded
denied
exclaimed
giggled
hesitated
hissed
hinted
hollered

muttered
nagged
objected
ordered
pleaded
promised
proclaimed
questioned
recalled
remembered
roared
scolded
scoffed
screamed
snarled
snorted
soothed
squawked
stammered
suggested
taunted
tattled
teased
whispered
whooped

Writing Time - Write a line of dialogue in each text box using other ways to say said.

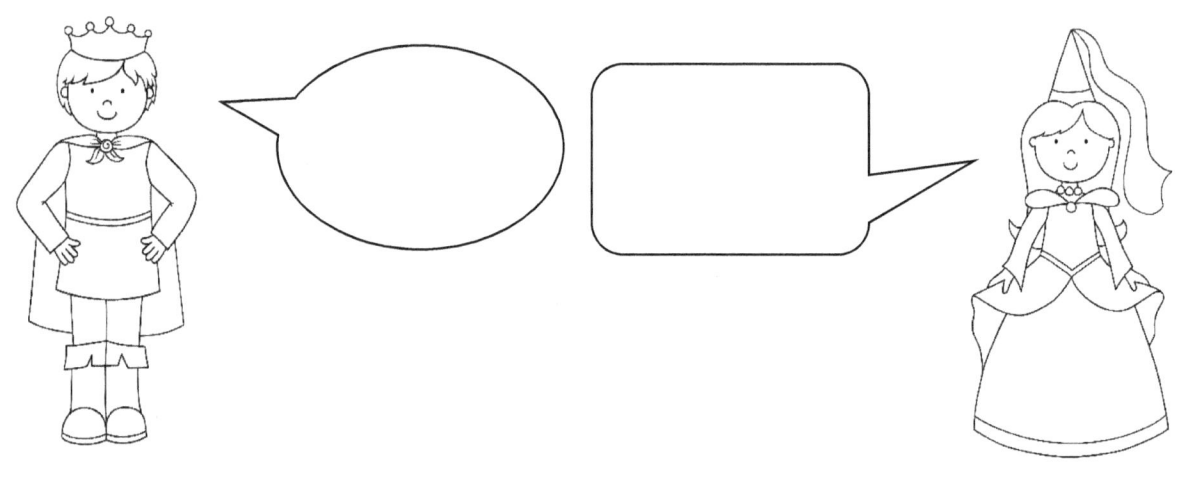

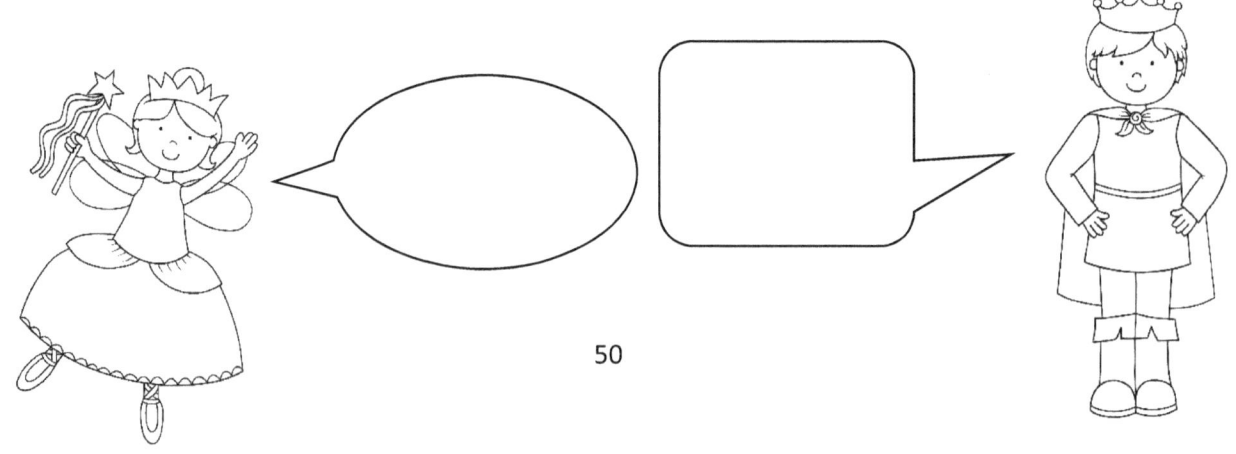

Princess School #5 – Forgiving is Beautiful!

We all have times in life when someone hurts us. If we don't forgive them it can turn into bitterness. When bitterness grows, it becomes an ugly grudge monster. By letting the hurt go and giving it to God, we stop it from growing into something ugly.

Copy the Bible verse: Ephesians 4:32, "Be kind and compassionate to one another, forgiving each other, just as in Christ God forgave you." (NIV)

_____
_____
_____
_____

Princess Homework

Write in your Princess Journal. Ask someone about a time they had to forgive and write about it in your Princess Journal.

Activity – Make Princess Hats

You will need:

- Inexpensive party hats from the dollar store, ones that point and have an elastic chin strap

- Fun and pretty wrapping or scrapbooking paper

- Tulle and ribbon in pretty princess colors, about a yard for each hat

- Jewels, stickers, or glitter to glue onto hat

Directions:

- Gently open and unfold each party hat and lay it on a sheet of construction paper. Trace around the hat with a pencil to use it for a pattern. Cut out the pattern.

- Lay the pattern on a piece of wrapping or scrapbooking paper that you would like to use to cover your hat. Trace around it with a marker. Cut it out and glue it to your hat with a glue stick. Glue the hat back together in a circle.

- Take 1-2 pieces of tulle and 1-2 pieces of ribbon and tie a knot on the end.

- Thread the piece of tulle through a hole in the top of the hat and pull. The knot should keep it from falling out.

- Decorate the hat with fun jewels and stickers.

Lesson Six

Show Don't Tell

Lesson Time

C.S. Lewis, the author of the popular Chronicles of Narnia, once said, "Don't tell me that your character is afraid.
Describe it in such a way that the very hairs on the back of my neck stand up when I read it." A good story describes the body language of the character's emotions, making the story come alive. This is the Golden Rule of Writing called "Show, Don't Tell."

Here are two examples of someone who is afraid.

1. Princess Piper ran along the dark hall. She heard a noise and was afraid. **These sentences TELL the reader she is afraid.**

2. Princess Piper ran along the dark hall. She heard a noise. Her heart pounded like a drum, and the hairs on the top of her head stood up. **These sentences SHOW the reader her body language when she was afraid.**

Can you see how the second sentence makes us experience her emotion?

Writing Time
Go on to the next page and fill in the handout.

Practice "Show, Don't Tell" Worksheet

Write a sentence for each emotion showing your character's body language as she experiences emotions. You can look at the examples on the previous page for help.

Excitement

_____
_____
_____

Fear

_____
_____
_____

Anger

_____
_____
_____

Happy

_____
_____
_____

You can also show other things like what kind of personality the princess has. For example, you can tell that the princess likes books, or you can show her reading them all the time.

Write a sentence showing that the princess is smart.

_____

_____

_____

Write a sentence showing that the princess is clumsy.

_____

_____

_____

Write a sentence showing that the princess is kind.

_____

_____

_____

Write a sentence showing that the princess doesn't like math.

_____

_____

_____

Princess School #6 *Believing in Yourself is Beautiful!*

You are special! Maybe you have brown eyes or blue, maybe you are short or tall. God made each person with just the right combination of gifts and talents that made Him happy. Maybe you can sing or play baseball. No one is exactly like you. You are unique! Even things you think may be unpleasant can turn out to be a blessing.

Copy the Bible Verse:
Psalm 139:14, "I praise you because I am fearfully and wonderfully made; your works are wonderful; I know that full well."
(NIV)

_____
_____
_____
_____

Princess Homework

Go to your "I Am Special" Itty-Bitty book in your Princess Diary. Draw a picture of yourself on the cover. Inside write ten things that make you special. Ask a parent for help.

"You Are Special" Name Art

Make this with your sister or best friend. Include fun photos of yourselves or special mementos.

You will need:

- Large and small stickers
- Wall-Art decals
- Small paper plates in various colors and patterns
- Magic (black) marker
- Alphabet stickers
- Puff paints or puff glue
- Wide ribbon (2-3 inches wide), 3 yards long for each
- Butterflies (plastic or sticker)
- Fun photos if desired

Choose the type and number of plates you want to use. Lay them out on the table or floor so you can see what they look like together. We chose a flowered plate to glue on top of a pink one in an alternate pattern.

Cut out the letters and pictures of the stickers you want to use, but don't peel and stick them yet, in case you want to change them around. Arrange them on the plates first to see how they look.

On the top plate, use the alphabet stickers and spell your name. Then decorate around it with stickers or glitter glue.

On the next plate, write what your name means, or write a Bible verse and decorate the plate.

Use large stickers that are sold for wall art to put in the middle of the next plate or draw a special word in glitter paint.

Roll out the ribbon and lay the plates on top of it in the order. Leave about two inches between each plate and four extra inches on top. With a hot glue gun, apply a couple of lines of glue right in the middle of the BACK of the plate. Be careful, it's hot! (Have a parent supervise.)

Then flip the plate over and attach it to the ribbon. We used the glue bottle to press it firmly in place because it was hot. Do this with all the plates. Tie a bow with the extra ribbon and attach it above the top plate on the ribbon with hot glue.

Writing Time – Continue writing your story. Skip a line.

Lesson Seven
Write the Middle and Strong Verbs

Lesson Time

All verbs show action, but not all verbs are the same in strength. "Wow words" are verbs that show a picture of what is going on and give your story punch. Weak verbs are overused and wimpy. They don't show much of anything.

For example, you could say, "The princess ran down the dark hall."

The verb is ran. If she was in a hurry or afraid, you could say that she "darted" or "bolted" down the hall. These words add a better picture of what she is doing.

A thesaurus is a helpful book of synonyms. It lists words that are similar to each other.

Use a thesaurus. Look up each verb below and write two stronger verbs. If you use computers, you can right-click on the word to find a drop-down box with synonyms.

Run _____   _____

Walk _____   _____

Carry _____   _____

Lift _____   _____

Crawl _____   _____

Bring _____   _____

Stronger Ways to Say Went

The word went is a weak verb. Try to use it as least as possible. Below are words to use instead of went. **Circle 10 words from** the list and see if you can change any "wents" in your story and replace them with the circled words.

Advanced	Fell	Rambled
Ambled	Flew	Retreated
Approached	Flitted	Roamed
Ascended	Floated	Rocketed
Barreled	Followed	Rushed
Blasted	Glided	Sailed
Bolted	Groveled	Scrambled
Boogied	Hastened	Scuttled
Bounced	Hightailed	Slithered
Bounded	Hiked	Staggered
Burst	Hoofed it	Stormed
Chugged	Hopped	Stumbled
Climbed	Hurdled	Traipsed
Crawled	Hurried	Vanished
Crept	Inched	Ventured
Cruised	Journeyed	Waddled
Danced	Loped	Wafted
Darted	Marched	Whisked
Dashed	Nosed	Zoomed

Lesson Time Continued

Write the Middle of Your Story

The middle of a story is where the character tries to solve the problem. It's even more exciting if the problem gets worse. Think drama, drama, drama! Some writers use the one, two, three method. The first two attempts to solve the problem fail, but on the third try, the character succeeds. It's like a thrilling roller coaster ride! First you go up, then down and upside down, but finally you come back down to the ground.

Writing Time – The "Build-Up" Creates Suspense

In this part of the story, your character tries to solve the problem but fails in the first several tries.

What is your story problem?

_____
_____

How does your character try to solve the problem?

_____
_____

How can you make the problem worse?

_____

Writing Time - Continue writing your story for 15-20 minutes on the next several pages. Remember to skip a line so you can add in things later.

Color the picture. Will the frog turn into a prince? You decide!

Activity - Make Princess Friendship Bracelets

You will need:

- 1 or 2 Empty toilet paper rolls
- Washi sticky tape with patterns found at a craft store
- Glitter glue, plastic craft gems, or initial stickers

Directions:

- Measure 2 – 3-inch segments of a toilet paper roll (whichever fit your wrists better)
- Then cut all around the toilet paper on the dotted line above.
- Then using washi tape – tape around the roll
- Then decorate with glitter, gems, crown, or initial stickers
- When dry, cut down the middle and trim to make it fit as a slip-on bracelet
- Give one to your BFF
- Instead of using washi tape you can also try painting the tubes, gluing wrapping paper, or foil around the tubes before you decorate

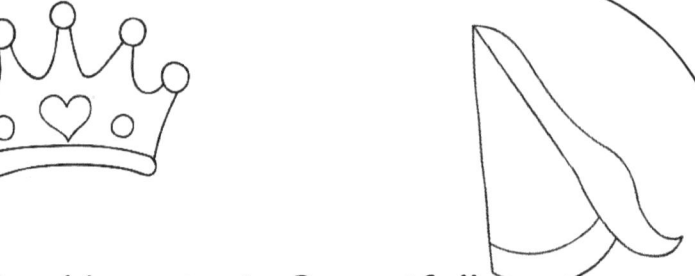

Princess School #7 – Honesty is Beautiful!

When a girl is honest, she is respected and will have a good reputation with others. Sometimes girls lie because they want something they can't wait for, so they manipulate the things and people around them to get it. It's better to trust God for the things and friendships we need. He will do a far better job at giving us what fulfills us. Sometimes girls lie because they are afraid of punishment. God forgives us when we make mistakes if we ask Him, and others will too if we are honest. God blesses those who are honest, so don't be afraid to tell the truth!

Copy the Bible verse:

Ephesians 4:25, "Therefore each of you must put off falsehood and speak truthfully to your neighbor, for we are all members of one body." (NIV)

_____

_____

_____

Princess Homework

Ask a parent or grandparent about a time when they did not want to be honest but were anyway. What happened? Did they feel better about it? Write their answers in your journal and what you think about what they said.

Lesson Eight
Personification

Lesson Time - Personification is giving person-like qualities to non-living things. Like: The pink flowers danced in the morning breeze. Flowers can't really dance but it gives a word picture in the story that the flowers were swaying in the breeze. It makes the story more exciting! On the lines below write a sentence giving each object human qualities.

A magic harp:

_____
_____
_____

A silver mirror:

_____
_____
_____

An apple tree:

_____
_____
_____

Writing Time – Write 15-20 minutes of your story today on the following pages. Include several uses of personification. Remember to add tension by letting your characters struggle a bit before they reach their goal.

Princess School #8 – *Generosity is Beautiful!*

Have you ever met someone who is stingy? They aren't very pleasant to be around. Being generous means being willing to give our time, talents, and our treasure to help someone else. There is a special blessing of feeling happy when we give to others! When we are generous, we are like our heavenly Father who gives generously to all men. Giving to others is like planting seeds. After a while, the seeds grow into fruit that we can enjoy too.

Copy the Bible verse:

Luke 6:38-40, "Give, and it will be given to you. A good measure, pressed down, shaken together and running over, will be poured into your lap." (NIV)

_____

_____

_____

Princess Homework

Write in your journal about a time someone shared with you and how that made you feel. OR write about a time when someone would NOT share and how that made you feel.

Activity – Share Your Time, Talents, and Treasure

Here are some ways you can practice generosity by giving your time, talent, or treasure:

Share your treasure by sharing food with a homeless shelter or food pantry. Share your toys with a children's hospital or family who needs them.

Share your time by helping a grandparent or elderly neighbor. You could walk someone's dog or do some chores.

Share your talents by helping a younger sibling or friend with their homework. You could read to a younger sibling or play your instrument to cheer someone up. Knit gloves or scarves for a homeless shelter.

List Five Other Ways You Can Be Generous

_____
_____
_____
_____
_____

Lesson Nine
Spice Up Your Story with Adjectives

Lesson Time

An adjective is a word that describes a noun.

A noun is a person, place, or thing.

Write an adjective in each of the blanks below for practice:

1. Princess Mia smelled the _____ flowers in the _____ tree.
2. The _____ horse galloped across the _____ field.
3. The _____ princess dashed to her _____ room.
4. Frankie the _____ frog, hopped up to the _____ princess.
5. Princess Sophia paints _____ pictures of the _____ castle lawn.
6. The two _____ girls ran across the _____ meadow.
7. When Princess Piper finished riding her _____ horse, she led him to the _____ barn.
8. The _____ princess shot the _____ arrows in the target.
9. The _____ princess hid when she heard a _____ noise.
10. The princess liked to sneak into the _____ kitchen and make a batch of _____ chocolate chip cookies.

Writing Time - Go to the first two pages of your story and circle the nouns. (No pronouns or names) Then add an adjective above them.

When you are finished, go on and write 15-20 minutes of your story. Remember to add some adjectives as you go!

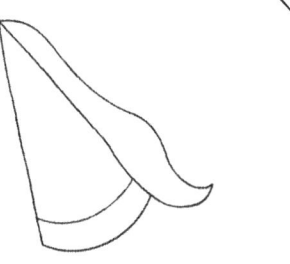

Princess School #9 - Diligence is Beautiful!

Being diligent means to keep working at something even if it's not easy. It's an important ingredient for succeeding in whatever you do. Don't give up easily. It's ok, if you need to rest a minute, just get back to it.

Copy the Bible verse:

"Diligent hands will rule, but laziness ends in forced labor." Proverbs 24:12 (NIV)

_____
_____
_____
_____

Princess Homework

Ask a parent about a time in their life when they worked diligently for something. What was it? Was it worth it? Write about it in your journal.

Activity – Write for the *Fairytale Gazette*

Help your fairytale community by starting a *Fairytale Gazette* newspaper. In the spaces on the next page is a newspaper worksheet. Fill it in by writing about what is happening in your village. The small spaces are to draw pictures of the event. The large spaces are for reporting what is happening. Here are some ideas: Report on activities, fairs, weddings, and birthday banquets of royalty. Report about who came to the event, what they ate, the princess gowns, and if there were any presents. Remember to use adjectives to help the reader see in their minds what you see.

Date:

Edition:

Fairytale Gazette

Date:

Edition:

Fairytale Gazette

Lesson Ten

Write the End of the Story

Lesson Time

Ending a story is helping the characters solve the story problem. If you want your character to learn a good life lesson, then it's also time to give them an "ah ha" moment, where they realize they have learned something.

Writing Time – On the next several pages finish your story. If you need more paper, go to the back of the book for extra pages.

Activity – Illustrate a Scene from Your Story

On a plain piece of white paper draw your character doing something in the story. This is called illustrating the story. Color it and set it aside to add to your story pages. Draw more if you like!

Princess School #10 – *Thinking of Others is Beautiful!*

A person who thinks about others realizes that everything is not always about them. The world is a big place, and we must take turns getting our way. If we always get our way, that means someone else is not getting their way. An unselfish person who cares about the feelings of others is truly beautiful and will be a person others want to be around. Unselfishness is beautiful!

Copy the Bible verse:

Philippians 2:4, "Let each of you look not only to his own interests but also to the interests of others." (ESV)

_____

_____

_____

Princess Homework

Practice letting someone else have their way today.

Finish your story here. Remember to skip a line. There are more pages at the back of the book if you need them.

Lesson Eleven
Editing

To edit means to correct any errors and change things to make the story better. Many great writers revise their stories ten to twenty times! We will only do it once. Here is a checklist to help:

_____1. Does every sentence begin with a capital letter and end with a period, question mark, or exclamation point?

_____2. Check your spelling with your parent.

_____3. Have you capitalized all the names of people and cities?

_____4. Do you have too many went words? If so, go back and change some into stronger verbs.

_____5. Can you add five more adjectives somewhere in your story?

_____ 6 Have you used all five senses in describing the setting somewhere in your story?

- Sights _____
- Sounds _____
- Tastes _____
- Textures_____
- Smells _____

_____7. Did you use personification twice in your story?

_____8. Do you have too many "said" words? If so, replace some with more exciting dialogue tag lines.

_____9. Did you use "Show Don't Tell" somewhere?

_____10. Completed all the above!

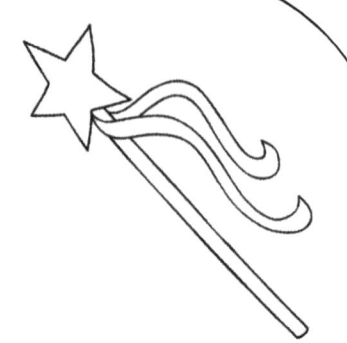

Princess School #11 - *Hospitality is Beautiful!*

Many people feel lonely, especially elderly people who live alone. People who just moved to your area feel lonely too. Sharing your home with others by providing food, a happy atmosphere, or lodging for the night can make others feel loved. Making special food always makes guests feel happy. Are there any foods you like preparing or would like to learn to prepare?

Copy the Bible verse below:

Hebrews 13:2" Do not forget to show hospitality to strangers, for by so doing some people have shown hospitality to angels without knowing it." (NIV)

_____

_____

_____

_____

Princess Homework

Invite someone that might be lonely over. Make special foods for them to enjoy. Try the princess cupcakes on the next page.

Activity – Bake Princess Cupcakes

- Make a batch of cupcakes as directed on the box of a <u>cake mix</u> of your favorite flavor. After cooling, frost with <u>vanilla frosting</u>.

- Frost <u>sugar cones</u> in vanilla or <u>strawberry</u> <u>frosting</u>, enough cones for each cupcake to have one. Then roll them in <u>pink sugar</u> or <u>pink sprinkles</u>.

- Place one cone upside down on top of each cupcake to make it look like the turret of a castle.

- Place <u>pink marshmallows</u>, <u>jellybeans, or colored chocolate candies</u> around the cone.

- Pipe hearts in the front or initials of special friends.

- Cut flags and hearts out of <u>red fruit roll-up</u> to stick on with frosting

Lesson Twelve

Put It All Together

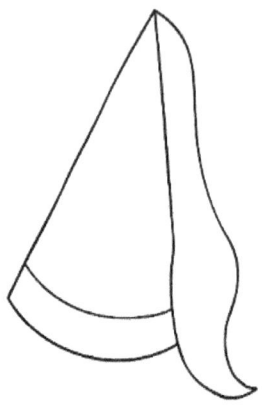

Color the title page and add a catchy title on the next page.

Tear out the final written story from this book and trim off any ragged edges. Number the pages. Use a three-hole punch to punch all the story pages and illustrations. Then place it into a plastic essay binder. These can be found at a superstore or office supply store. If you want a short cut, just staple the pages together.

Activity - Fairytale Flashlight Theatre

Choose a table or comfy family room chair to be your stage. Turn out the lights and flash several flashlights on the reader as each student takes turns reading their stories. For a fun option, cut out a large square from a large box making it look like a TV. Add paint or glitter. Make popcorn or another fun snack. Have the reader sit behind it and read. As an option, let them dress up in fun costumes, hats, or glasses. This is always a highlight! Share good flashlight behavior beforehand: No flashing in anyone's eyes or waving them around to make fun patterns on the wall. Invite grandparents, friends, or neighbors. You can even invite other siblings or friends to read their stories too!

_____

By

_____

Fairytale Theater

Make Pretty Princess Popcorn

- Pop two bags of microwave popcorn. Dump in a big bowl.

- In a microwave-safe bowl, dump one package of white or milk chocolate chips. Microwave thirty seconds at a time, stirring each time. (About two-three times) When you can stir it until it's smooth, pour over popcorn.

- Top with pink sprinkles right away!

- Add nuts, marshmallows, or other candies right away so they stick together.

Activity – Draw a Scene

Draw a scene from your story. Maybe it's a picture of your princess. Maybe it's a map of the village. Maybe the princess is doing something she loves.

Activity – Draw a Scene

Draw a scene from your story. Maybe it's a picture of your princess. Maybe it's a map of the village. Maybe the princess is doing something she loves.

Creative Writing Made Easy . . . Helping Every Child Succeed

About the Author

Jan May loved homeschooling her two children through high school. Whether it was hosting a dress-up mystery club, or collecting an amphibian zoo, hands-on education was always at the forefront of her curriculum. She is the author of the *Creative Writing Made Easy* series that engages even the most reluctant writers. All of the books are filled with fun, interactive activities involving each type of learner: visual, auditory, and kinesthetic. They are perfect for the wiggle in boys and perfect for craft-loving girls! Having been a creative writing teacher for over fifteen years, Jan believes that given the right tools, every child can learn to write and love it!

Visit her website for fun activities. Watch for her online teaching schedule—leading students and teens in a fun and engaging writing experience. www.NewMillenniumGirlBooks.com.

If you enjoyed this book, you might also enjoy: *Isabel Writing Bundle – Write with Isabel and her horse Starlight.* One mom said, "My daughter was a storyteller but couldn't get it out on paper until we found these books. It turned writing time into a delight!" A. Blevins

www.ingramcontent.com/pod-product-compliance
Lightning Source LLC
Chambersburg PA
CBHW061112070526
44583CB00027B/3270